SILAS MARNER

In the quiet villages of England in the early nineteenth century, life follows an unchanging pattern. The seasons come and go, for both the rich Squire and his family in the big house, and the villagers in their little cottages. Anything new or strange is met with suspicion in villages like Raveloe.

And Silas Marner the linen-weaver *is* strange. He lives alone, and no one knows anything about his family. How can you trust a man when you don't know his mother and father? And he is pale, with strange, staring eyes, for he works long hours at his loom every day – even on Sundays, when he should be in church. He must be a friend of the devil, the villagers say to each other.

Poor Silas! He's a sad, lonely man, and his only friends are the bright gold coins that he earns for his weaving and keeps hidden under the floorboards. But change must come, even to a quiet place like Raveloe. The Squire's two sons share a secret, which leads to quarrelling, robbery, and a death, one cold snowy night not far from the door of Silas's cottage . . .

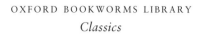

OXFORD BOOKWORMS LIBRARY

Classics

Silas Marner

Stage 4 (1400 headwords)

Series Editor: Jennifer Bassett
Founder Editor: Tricia Hedge
Activities Editors: Jennifer Bassett and Alison Baxter

GEORGE ELIOT

Silas Marner
The Weaver of Raveloe

Retold by
Clare West

OXFORD UNIVERSITY PRESS

OXFORD
UNIVERSITY PRESS

Great Clarendon Street, Oxford OX2 6DP

Oxford University Press is a department of the University of Oxford.
It furthers the University's objective of excellence in research, scholarship,
and education by publishing worldwide in

Oxford New York

Auckland Cape Town Dar es Salaam Hong Kong Karachi
Kuala Lumpur Madrid Melbourne Mexico City Nairobi
New Delhi Shanghai Taipei Toronto

With offices in

Argentina Austria Brazil Chile Czech Republic France Greece
Guatemala Hungary Italy Japan Poland Portugal Singapore
South Korea Switzerland Thailand Turkey Ukraine Vietnam

OXFORD and OXFORD ENGLISH are registered trade marks of
Oxford University Press in the UK and in certain other countries

ISBN 978 0 19 479184 7

A complete recording of this Bookworms edition of
Silas Marner is available.

Typeset by Wyvern Typesetting Ltd, Bristol

Printed in China

ACKNOWLEDGEMENTS
Illustrated by: Susan Scott

Word count (main text): 16,065 words

For more information on the Oxford Bookworms Library,
visit www.oup.com/elt/bookworms

CONTENTS

— 1 —
Silas Marner, past and present

In the early years of the nineteenth century, strange-looking little men were often seen on the country roads, usually with a heavy bag on their shoulders. They were linen-weavers, taking the linen they had woven to the women in the villages. Unlike the strong, healthy country people, they were small and thin, with tired white faces, bent backs and round shoulders. They were often shortsighted too, because they had to look so closely at their work. To the villagers the weavers looked almost foreign, and quite frightening. Where did they come from? Was it the devil who sent them? Who were their parents? How could you trust a man if you didn't know his father or mother? Country people used to be very suspicious of all strangers and travellers. They were also suspicious of clever people, people who could do something they themselves had not learnt to do. That is why the linen-weavers, who often moved from towns to live and work in the country, were considered strangers all their lives by their neighbours, and were sometimes very lonely as a result.

Silas Marner was one of these weavers. He lived in a small cottage near the village of Raveloe. Every day he worked at his loom in the cottage. The small boys of Raveloe had never heard the sound of a loom before, and sometimes they used to run up to his house to look quickly in at the window. If Silas noticed them, he lifted his shortsighted eyes from the loom to stare at the boys. There was something terrible about his stare, which made the boys run away at once, screaming with fear. The villagers believed that Silas had an almost devilish power, which he could use to harm them if he wanted, and so they were all afraid of him. Raveloe was an important-looking village with a fine old church and a number of large farms. But it was at least an hour away from any other village, and very few strangers visited it, which explains why the villagers' opinions were so out of date.

Silas Marner had first come to Raveloe fifteen years before, as a young man. He and his way of life seemed very strange to the villagers. He worked long hours at his loom, and had no friends or visitors from the village or anywhere else. He never talked to his neighbours unless it was necessary for his work, and he never looked at any of the Raveloe girls. 'Who would want to marry him anyway?' the girls laughed to each other. 'Marry a dead man come to life again, with that unhealthy white skin and those insect-like eyes of his? Certainly not!'

One of the villagers had had a strange experience with Silas. One evening he had discovered the weaver resting on a field gate, his eyes open but unseeing, and his body cold and hard, like a dead man's. After a few moments Silas appeared to wake up, said 'Goodnight', and walked away.

When this was discussed in the village, some people thought that Silas had had a fit. But others, like Mr Macey, the church clerk, refused to accept a medical explanation.

'No, he isn't ill, that weaver,' said old Mr Macey, shaking his head knowingly. 'If he had a fit, he'd fall down, wouldn't he? I think his soul flies out of his body sometimes and that's why he looks so strange. He doesn't come to church, does he? And how does he know so much about medicines? You all remember how he made Sally Oates better, when the doctor himself could do no more for her. That's the devil's work, believe me!'

However, the housewives needed Silas to weave their linen, and they could find nothing wrong with his work. The years passed, and Raveloe villagers did not change their opinion of the weaver. At the end of fifteen years they said exactly the same things about him, but they believed them more strongly. They also said that he had saved up a lot of money since he had come to Raveloe.

Silas had come from a large town to the north of Raveloe. Here he had lived a very different life. Because he was one of a large number of weavers, he was not considered strange, and he belonged to an enthusiastic religious group. They met every Sunday at the chapel in Light Street. Once, at a chapel meeting, Silas had become unconscious and had sat without moving, hearing or seeing, for over an hour. This experience made him specially interesting to the rest of the group.

'We should not call this strange unconsciousness a fit,' the minister, Mr Paston, told them. 'No, it's much more than that. In that moment, when he is absent from us, our young friend Silas's soul is *open*, open to a possible message from God. I believe he has been chosen by God!'

Silas's best friend at chapel was William Dane, a serious young man who was, some people thought, a little too sure of his own goodness and cleverness. Silas, however, could see no fault in him, and trusted his friend completely. They remained

*Once, at a chapel meeting, Silas had been unconscious
for over an hour.*

good friends, when Silas became engaged to a young woman, Sarah, who belonged to the same chapel. In fact Silas was delighted that Sarah did not mind if William joined them sometimes on their Sunday walks.

Strangely, when Silas had his fit at the chapel meeting, William was the only one who disagreed with the minister.

'To me it looks more like the devil's work than God's,' William had said. 'Look deep into yourself, friend Silas. Is there any evil hiding in your soul?'

Silas was hurt that his friend doubted him, and he began to be worried, too, about Sarah. She seemed to be showing signs of dislike towards him, but when he asked her about it, she did not give him any answer.

At that time one of the chapel leaders was dangerously ill, and because he had no family, some of the young men offered to sit with him at night. One night Silas was sitting alone at the old man's bedside. Time seemed to pass slowly in the quiet, dark room. But suddenly he realized that the man was no longer breathing. He was dead.

'Strange!' thought Silas. 'His body's cold! He's been dead for some time! Why didn't I notice? Perhaps I've had another fit. And it's already four o'clock in the morning. Why hasn't William come? He promised he'd come at two o'clock!' He hurried out of the house to call the doctor and the minister, and then went to work as usual, still wondering why William had not arrived.

But that evening, after work, William came to his room, with the minister. They were both looking very serious.

'You must come to the chapel at once,' said Mr Paston.

'But why?' asked Silas, looking unhappily at them.

'You will hear when you get there,' was the only answer.

Then, in the chapel, Silas stood alone, in front of all the people who were once his friends. The room was silent. There was a pocket-knife in the minister's hand.

'Where did you leave this knife?' he asked.

Silas was trembling at this strange question. 'I don't remember,' he answered.

'Silas, Silas, you must confess!' cried the minister. 'Tell us the truth! This knife, *your* knife, was found at the dead man's bedside, and the bag of church money, which I saw there myself only yesterday, has gone!'

Silas did not speak for a moment. Then he said, 'God knows I did not steal the money. Search my room – you won't find the money. I'm not a thief.'

'You were the only one in our dead friend's house last night, when the money was stolen,' said Mr Paston. 'William tells us he was suddenly ill, which prevented him from coming to take your place. We will search your room.'

And when they went to Silas's room, William found the missing bag, now empty, under Silas's bed.

'Silas, my friend,' cried William, 'confess your crime to us now! Send the devil away from your soul!'

Silas turned to the man he had always trusted. 'William, in the nine years since we've been friends, have I ever told you a lie? But God will prove the truth.'

As he looked at William, he suddenly remembered something,

and reddened. He said in a trembling voice, 'The knife wasn't in my pocket last night!'

'I don't know what you mean,' replied William coldly.

In the strange little world of the Light Street chapel, they did not believe in the law or judges. They thought only God knew the answers, so they agreed to draw lots to decide what had happened. They all went down on their knees to ask for God's help in finding the truth. Silas knelt with them, sure that God would prove his honesty. There was silence, as the minister took one of the papers out of the covered box.

'*The lots say that Silas Marner has stolen the money,*' he said. 'You will leave the chapel, Silas Marner, and you will not be accepted back until you confess your crime.'

Silas listened in horror. At last he walked over to William Dane and said firmly, 'I lent you my knife, you know that. *You* stole the money, while I was having a fit, and you've blamed me for it. But perhaps you'll never be punished, since there is no God who takes care of the good and punishes the bad, only a God of lies.'

'You hear, my friends?' said William, smiling sadly. 'This is the voice of the devil speaking.'

Silas went home. The next day he sat alone for the whole day, too miserable to do anything. On the second day the minister came to tell him that Sarah had decided she could not marry him. Only a month later, Sarah married William Dane, and soon afterwards Silas Marner left the town.

At Raveloe, Silas shut himself away in his cottage. He did not want to think about the disaster he had experienced. He could not understand why God had refused to help him. But now that his trust in God and his friends had been broken, he did not feel strong enough to build up that trust again, in a new church and with new friends. From now on, he would live in a dark, loveless, hopeless world.

All that was left to him was his weaving, and he sat at his loom seven days a week, working all the daylight hours. In the town he had earned less, and had given much of his money to the chapel, for the old, the poor, and the sick. But now he began to earn more than ever before, and there was no reason for him to give away any of it. He was often paid for his linen in gold. He discovered that he liked holding the shining coins in his hand and looking at their bright faces.

In his childhood, Silas had been taught, by his mother, to make simple medicines from wild flowers and plants. One day he saw the shoemaker's wife, Sally Oates, sitting at her cottage door, and he realized she had all the signs of the illness which had killed his mother. He felt sorry for Sally, and although he knew he could not prevent her dying, he prepared some medicine for her which made her feel much better. The villagers considered this a good example of Silas's strange, frightening power, but as it had worked for Sally, they started visiting Silas to ask for help with their own illnesses. But Silas was too honest to take their money and give them useless medicine. He knew he had no special power, and so he sent them away. The villagers believed he was refusing to help them, and they were angry with him. They blamed him for accidents that happened to them, and deaths in the village. So poor Silas's

Silas liked holding the shining gold coins in his hand.

kindness to Sally did not help him make friends in Raveloe.

But little by little, the piles of gold coins in his cottage grew higher. The harder he worked, the less he spent on himself. He counted the coins into piles of ten, and wanted to see them grow into a square, and then into a larger square. He was delighted with every new coin, but it made him want another. His gold became a habit, a delight, a reason for living, almost a religion. He began to think the coins were his friends, who made the cottage less lonely for him. But it was only at night, when he had finished his work, that he spent time with them. He kept them in two bags, under the floorboards near the loom. Like a thirsty man who needs a drink, he took them out every evening to look at them, feel them, and count them. The coins shone in the firelight, and Silas loved every one of them. When he looked at his loom, he thought fondly of the half-earned gold in the work he was doing, and he looked forward to the years ahead of him, the countless days of weaving and the growing piles of gold.

— 2 —

Godfrey and Dunstan Cass

The most important person in Raveloe was Squire Cass, a gentleman farmer, who lived with his three sons in the handsome red house opposite the church, and owned a number of farms outside the village. His wife had died many years before.

One dark November evening, fifteen years after Silas Marner had first arrived in Raveloe, some of the villagers were drinking beer in the public house, the Rainbow. Old Mr Macey, the church clerk, was remembering the Squire's wife.

'She was a wonderful lady,' he said, shaking his grey head sadly. 'Everything was always so pretty and clean at the Red House when she was alive! When she died, all those years ago, the poor Squire, well, he didn't know *what* to do. And he's still lonely, believe me! That's why we often see him in here in the evenings. And another thing, if poor Mrs Cass were alive today, I'm sure she'd be very disappointed with her sons. The Squire should make those boys do some work, but instead he lets them stay at home and gives them money to spend on horses, or gambling, or women!'

'Come, come, Mr Macey,' said the landlord. 'They're rich young gentlemen, after all. You can't expect them to work on the farms like us country people. But you're right about Dunstan Cass. He's a bad one, he is. Always borrowing money, and never paying it back. Always gambling, always in trouble! He'll come to a bad end, he will!'

'But the other two are different,' said the butcher, a red-faced, smiling man. 'Bob Cass is still only a boy. And Mr Godfrey, the eldest, well, I don't believe he'll be like his brother Dunstan. Just look at him! He's got an open, honest face. And he's going to inherit the Squire's money and all the land. And what's more, he's going to marry Miss Nancy Lammeter. When she moves into the Red House as Mrs Godfrey Cass, she'll make life more comfortable for all the Casses. She'll save the Squire money too

– the Lammeters have the best of everything in their house, but they're very careful with their money.'

The farrier, a small man with a sharp face, always enjoyed disagreeing with the butcher. 'Mr Godfrey marry Miss Nancy!' he laughed. 'That's what *you* think! Haven't you noticed how Miss Nancy has changed towards Godfrey since last year? You remember, he was away from home, for days and days. Nobody knows what he was doing, but Godfrey hasn't been the same since then. Miss Nancy isn't stupid – she won't marry a man she can't trust!'

The landlord always tried to prevent his customers from arguing. 'What you all say is very true. But let's hope that Mr Godfrey doesn't lose his chance of marrying Miss Nancy.'

Meanwhile, at the Red House, Godfrey Cass was waiting for his brother in the sitting-room, with a very worried expression on his handsome face. Soon the door opened, and a heavy-looking young man entered. It was Dunstan. He had clearly been drinking.

'How I hate him!' thought Godfrey.

'Well, *sir*,' said Dunstan unpleasantly, 'you sent for me, and as you're the oldest, and you'll be the Squire one day, I have to obey you. So what do you want?'

'Just listen, will you?' replied Godfrey angrily, 'if you aren't too drunk to understand! You must pay me back the money I lent you last month. You know I got it from Fowler, of Church Farm. He owed the money to the Squire, and asked me to give it to him. Now the Squire is angry with Fowler for not paying, and I've *got* to give the money back!'

Dunstan came close to Godfrey and smiled in an evil way. 'Well, my dear kind brother, why don't you find the money *yourself*? That would be much less trouble for me!'

Godfrey controlled himself with difficulty. 'Don't smile at me like that, or I'll hit you!'

'Oh no, you won't,' answered Dunstan. 'Because if you do, I'll tell the Squire your secret. I'll tell him that his handsome eldest son fell in love with that poor girl Molly in the town, and married her in a hurry. The Squire'll be angry because you married her in secret, and he'll disinherit you. Then *I'll* get the house and land when the old man dies! But don't worry, I'm a good brother to you. I won't tell him, and you'll find the money to pay back, I know you will.'

'Where can I get the money from?' cried Godfrey. 'I tell you, I haven't got any!'

'You could borrow it,' said Dunstan carelessly. 'Or wait – I've had a better idea. You could sell your horse.'

'Sell Wildfire! You know how much I love that horse!'

'Well, you could ride him to the hunt tomorrow. I know two or three men who'd be interested in buying him, and they'll be at the hunt, I'm sure. It'd be easy.'

'No, I haven't got time to go hunting tomorrow. I – I'm going to Mrs Osgood's birthday dance.'

'Aha!' said Dunstan, laughing. 'And perhaps you'll see sweet Miss Nancy there – and you'll dance with her – and you'll talk of love . . .'

'Be quiet!' shouted Godfrey, his face turning red. 'Don't speak of Miss Nancy like that, or I'll kill you!'

Dunstan came close to Godfrey and smiled in an evil way.

'Don't get so angry, brother,' answered Dunstan calmly. 'You've got a very good chance with her. In fact, I advise you to be nice to her. You and I know that Molly's started drinking. Well, if she drinks too much one day and dies, then you could marry Nancy. She wouldn't mind being a second wife, if she didn't know there was a first. And luckily you've got a kind brother who'll keep your secret well.'

Godfrey's face was white now, and he was trembling. 'Look, Dunstan, I've nearly had enough of this. You can push a man too far, you know. Perhaps I'll go to the Squire now and confess everything to him. He'll discover the truth one day, because Molly says she'll come and tell him. She wants everyone to know we're married. When the Squire knows the truth, you won't get any more money from me!'

Dunstan replied lightly, 'Do what you like, brother.'

Godfrey hesitated. He knew he had fallen into Dunstan's trap, when he made the mistake of marrying Molly. It was Dunstan who had introduced his brother to Molly, hoping that Godfrey would fall in love and marry her. Dunstan was clearly delighted that his evil plan had succeeded. Godfrey was now in a difficult situation. He no longer loved his young wife, and could not stop thinking of Nancy Lammeter. He felt sure that with Nancy as his wife he would not need to have secrets, and could be open and honest with everybody. But for the moment he had to give Dunstan whatever he wanted, keep Molly happy, and lie to his father and his friends. If he told his father the truth, the situation would become impossible. The Squire would disinherit him and he would be just a poor working man for the rest of his life. And far worse than that, he would lose any hope of marrying Nancy. No! He could not accept that. He would find the money for Dunstan, and wait for the situation to get better. Living with fear in his heart, the fear of being discovered, was better than living without Nancy's love.

He turned to Dunstan. 'It's just like you to talk of selling Wildfire – the best horse I've ever had!'

'Let *me* sell him for you – you know I'm good at buying and selling. I can ride him to the hunt for you tomorrow, and bring you back the money. But you must decide. You lent me that money, and you'll have to pay it back to the Squire. So it's your problem, not mine!'

Godfrey thought for a moment. 'All right,' he said. 'But make sure you bring me back all the money, Dunstan!'

The next morning, as Dunstan was riding Wildfire out of Raveloe, he passed the old quarry. All the stone had been taken out of it and it was no longer used; now all that was left was a deep hole full of reddish water. Opposite the quarry was Silas Marner's cottage. Dunstan suddenly had an idea. 'Everybody in Raveloe talks of the weaver's money – he must have a lot hidden away in that cottage! Why doesn't Godfrey borrow some money from him, and pay him back when he becomes the Squire?' He wondered whether to go back to the Red House at once, to tell Godfrey about this wonderful idea of his, but he did not want to miss the hunt, so he decided to continue on his way.

At the hunt he met several friends and neighbours, and before the hunt started he managed to sell Wildfire for a good price.

The money would be paid when he brought the horse to the neighbour's house later that day. Dunstan knew it would be safer to take the horse there immediately, so that he could be sure of receiving the money. But he was confident that he could take care of Wildfire during the hunt, and so, after a glass or two of whisky, he joined the other riders in the fields. This time, however, he was not as lucky as usual, and horse and rider fell while jumping a gate. Dunstan got up, shaken but unhurt, but poor Wildfire's back was broken, and in a few moments he died.

Dunstan looked around, and was glad to see that no other riders had noticed his accident. He did not want people to think he was a bad rider. He did not care much about Wildfire, because he thought he now had a much better plan to offer Godfrey. The worst thing was that he would have to walk home, something he was not at all used to doing.

He drank some more whisky from the bottle he kept in his pocket, and started down the country road. He kept thinking about Silas's money. There would certainly be enough for his own needs as well as Godfrey's. Dunstan thought it would be easy to frighten the weaver a little, and then Silas would quickly agree to lend his money.

It was four o'clock in the afternoon, and the whole countryside was covered by a thick mist. Dunstan did not see anyone on his way back to Raveloe. He knew he was getting close to the old quarry, although he could not see the road in front of him. At last he saw light coming from the weaver's cottage, and he decided to knock at the door. 'Why not ask the old man for the money now?' he thought.

But when he knocked loudly, there was no reply. And when he pushed the door, it opened. Dunstan found himself in front of a bright fire which showed every corner of the small living-room. Silas Marner was not there. Dunstan was tired and cold, so he went quickly to sit by the warm fire. As he sat down, he noticed a small piece of meat cooking over the fire. It was hanging from a large door key.

'So, the old man's cooking meat for his supper, is he?' thought Dunstan. 'But where is he? Why is his door unlocked? Perhaps he went out to fetch some wood for the fire, and fell into the quarry! Perhaps he's dead!' This was an interesting new idea. 'And if he's dead, *who inherits his money? Who would know that anybody had come to take it away?*' And the most important question of all – '*Where is the money?*'

Dunstan's excitement made him forget that the weaver could still be alive. He wanted Silas to be dead, and he wanted Silas's money. He looked round the cottage again. There was very little furniture, just a bed, the loom, three chairs and a table. Dunstan looked under the bed, but the money was not there. Then he noticed a place on the floor, near the loom, where the floorboards looked different. By pulling up one of the boards, he discovered Silas's hiding-place. He took out the two heavy bags filled with gold, put the boards back and hurried to the door.

Outside, the rain was falling heavily, and he could not see anything at all. Carrying the heavy bags, he stepped forward into the darkness.

Carrying the heavy bags, Dunstan stepped forward into the darkness.

— 3 —
Where is Silas's gold?

When Dunstan Cass left the cottage, Silas Marner was only a hundred metres away. He was walking home from the village, where he had gone to buy what he needed for his next day's work. His legs were tired, but he felt almost happy. He was looking forward to supper-time, when he would bring out his gold. Tonight he had an extra reason to hurry home. He was going to eat hot meat, which was unusual for him. And it would cost him nothing, because someone had given him a piece of meat as a present. He had left it cooking over the fire. The door key was needed to hold it safely in place, but Silas was not at all worried about leaving his gold in the cottage with the door unlocked. He could not imagine that a thief would find his way through the mist, rain and darkness to the little cottage by the quarry.

When he reached his cottage and opened the door, he did not notice that anything was different. He threw off his wet coat, and pushed the meat closer to the fire. As soon as he was warm again, he began to think about his gold. It seemed a long time to wait until after supper, when he usually brought out the coins to look at. So he decided to bring out his gold immediately, while the meat was still cooking.

But when he took up the floorboards near the loom, and saw the empty hole, he did not understand at once. His heart beat violently as his trembling hands felt all round the hole. There was nothing there! He put his hands to his head and tried to

20

think. Had he put his gold in a different place, and forgotten about it? He searched every corner of his small cottage, until he could not pretend to himself any more. He had to accept the truth – his gold had been stolen!

He gave a wild, desperate scream, and stood still for a moment. Then he turned towards his loom, and almost fell into the seat where he always worked. He touched the loom to make sure it, too, had not been stolen. Now he was beginning to think more clearly. 'A thief has been here! If I can find him, he'll have to give back my gold! But I was only away for a short time, and there's no sign of anyone entering the cottage.' He wondered whether it was really a thief who had taken his money, or whether it was the same cruel God who had already destroyed his happiness once. But Silas preferred to suspect a thief, who would perhaps return the money. He began to think it must be Jem Rodney, a local poacher, who had known about Silas's money, and who sometimes visited the cottage. Silas felt stronger now that he thought he knew the thief. 'I must go and tell the Squire, and the police!' he said to himself. 'They'll make Jem give me back the money!' So he hurried out in the rain without a coat, and ran towards the Rainbow.

He thought he would find the most important people in Raveloe at the public house, but in fact most of them were at Mrs Osgood's birthday dance. There were, however, five villagers at the Rainbow, enjoying an interesting conversation about ghosts, while drinking their beer.

'I tell you, people *have* seen ghosts,' the butcher said. 'And I'll tell you where, too. Behind the church!'

'That's right,' agreed old Mr Macey. 'You young ones aren't old enough to remember, but people have seen ghosts near the church since I was a boy. Oh yes, it's true.'

The farrier laughed scornfully. 'Ghosts! People *imagine* they see things on a dark night! You can't make *me* believe in ghosts! It's a question of fact! There are no ghosts!'

'Now, now,' began the landlord, who always tried to keep the peace, 'in some ways you're all wrong, and in some ways you're all right, that's my opinion. There *are* ghosts, and there *aren't*, well, that's what people say. And . . .'

Just then Silas's white face appeared suddenly in the doorway. He had run all the way from his cottage, so he could not speak for a moment. He stared silently at the men with his strange staring eyes, looking exactly like a ghost. For a few minutes nobody said anything, while Silas tried to control his breathing. Then the landlord spoke.

'What do you want, Master Marner? Come, tell us.'

'Robbed!' cried Silas, suddenly able to speak. 'I've been robbed! I want the police, and the Squire!' He waved his arms wildly as he spoke.

'Hold him, Jem,' said the landlord to the poacher, who was sitting near the door. 'I think he's gone mad.'

But Jem moved quickly away. 'Not me!' he replied. 'I don't want anything to do with a ghost!'

'Jem Rodney!' cried Silas, turning and staring at the man he suspected.

'Yes, Master Marner?' answered Jem, trembling a little.

'If it was you who stole my money,' said Silas, going close to

Jem, 'just give it back to me, and I won't tell the police. Please – just give it back.'

'Stole your money!' cried Jem angrily. 'I'll throw this glass at you if you accuse me of stealing your money!'

'Come now, Master Marner,' said the landlord firmly, taking Silas by the arm. 'You must explain what you mean if you want us to believe you. And sit down by the fire to dry your clothes. You're very wet.'

'That's right,' said the farrier. 'No more staring like a madman. That's what I thought you were at first – not a ghost, of course.'

The weaver sat down, in the centre of the little group of men, and told his story. It felt strange but pleasant to him, to talk to his neighbours and tell them his problems. The men realized at once that Silas was telling the truth. They had suspected him of working for the devil, but they knew now that the devil was no longer taking care of him.

'Well, Master Marner,' said the landlord in the end, 'you mustn't accuse poor Jem. He sometimes steals a chicken, we all know that, but he's been sitting here drinking with us all evening. So he's not the thief.'

'That's right,' said old Mr Macey. 'You can't accuse someone who hasn't done anything wrong, Master Marner.'

These words brought the past back to Silas, and he remembered standing in front of his accusers in the Light Street chapel. He went up to Jem.

'I was wrong,' he said miserably. 'I'm sorry, Jem. I had no reason to accuse you. But – where can my gold be?'

The weaver sat down and told his story.

'Perhaps some stranger came to your cottage while you were out,' said the farrier. 'But we must report the robbery to the police and the Squire immediately.'

Next morning, when the whole village heard about the stolen gold, they all discussed it excitedly. A few people still did not trust Silas or believe his story. Most people, however, were suspicious of the pedlar who had visited Raveloe the month before. Perhaps he had returned to hide near the quarry, and steal the money when Silas left his cottage. Several villagers thought they remembered his evil-looking face, and felt sure he was not honest.

Silas himself remembered that the pedlar had come to his cottage door recently. He hoped the pedlar was indeed the thief, because the police could catch him and make him give back the money. His home seemed very empty to him without his gold, and he desperately wanted to get it back.

— 4 —
Godfrey is in trouble

Godfrey was not very surprised to find that Dunstan had not come home after his day's hunting. Perhaps he was staying the night at a public house. But when Dunstan did not return home the next day, Godfrey began to worry about Wildfire. He did not trust his brother, and wondered if Dunstan had gone away to spend the money on gambling. So he decided to go to look for him. On the road near Raveloe he met his neighbour, John

Bryce, who had arranged to buy Wildfire from Dunstan.

'Well, Godfrey,' said Bryce, 'did your brother tell you about the horse?'

'What do you mean, John?' replied Godfrey quickly. 'No, he hasn't been home yet. What's happened to my horse?'

'Ah, so he was yours, was he? Dunstan told me you'd *given* him Wildfire. I was going to buy him, you know.'

'What's Dunstan done? Is Wildfire hurt?' asked Godfrey crossly.

'Worse than that,' answered Bryce. 'I'm afraid your horse is dead. We've only just found him. Your brother rode him to the hunt and the horse fell at a gate and broke his back. So you haven't seen Dunstan since yesterday?'

'No, and he'd better not come home now!' replied Godfrey angrily. 'How stupid I was to trust him with my horse!'

'But where can Dunstan be? I suppose he wasn't hurt, because we didn't find him near the horse.'

'Him?' said Godfrey bitterly. 'Oh, he'll be all right. He'll never be hurt – he only ever hurts other people! We'll hear of him soon enough, don't worry.'

Bryce said goodbye and rode away. Godfrey rode slowly back into Raveloe, thinking about what he would very soon have to do. There was no longer any escape. He must confess the whole truth to his father. For the rest of the day he planned what he would say. He would explain that he had lent Fowler's money to Dunstan, because Dunstan knew his secret. That would be the right moment to tell the Squire about his secret marriage to Molly. 'But he'll be very angry!' thought Godfrey.

'And when he's angry with people, he just wants to punish them! He won't listen or calm down! But perhaps he'll keep my secret – he's so proud of the family name! And if he disinherited me, everyone would talk about it.'

When he went to bed that night, Godfrey thought he had decided what to say. But when he woke up in the morning, he could not see any reason to confess to the marriage. Why should he lose the chance of marrying Nancy? Why should he tell the whole truth now, when perhaps it was not necessary? No, it would be better to go on in the same way as before. Perhaps Dunstan would stay away for a while, and then there would be no need to tell his father about Molly. 'But today I'll tell the Squire about the money,' he thought. 'He'll have to know about *that.*'

Godfrey was already in the dining-room when his father arrived for breakfast. The Squire sat down at the head of the table and ordered the servant to bring him some beer.

'Haven't you had breakfast yet, Godfrey?' he asked.

'Yes, I have, sir,' replied Godfrey, 'but I was waiting to speak to you.'

'Well, you young people have plenty of time,' answered the Squire. 'We older ones have to do all the work.'

Godfrey looked straight at his father. 'Sir,' he said bravely, 'I must tell you – something very unfortunate has happened to Wildfire.'

'What! Has he broken a leg? I thought you could ride better than that! Well, you can't expect me to pay for a new horse. I'm very short of money at the moment. And I'm angry with Fowler

– he *still* hasn't paid me what he owes me. If he doesn't pay today, he'll go to prison!' The Squire's face was red, and he banged angrily on the table as he spoke.

'It's worse than breaking a leg,' continued Godfrey miserably. 'Wildfire's dead. But I don't want you to buy me another horse. I just feel sorry I can't pay you – you see, sir, the truth is, I'm very sorry, Fowler *did* pay the money. He gave it to me, and I was stupid enough to let Dunstan have it. And he was going to sell Wildfire and then I was going to repay you the money.'

The Squire's face was purple now, and for a moment he could not speak. 'You – you let Dunstan have my money? *Why* did you give it to him? And why did he want it? Where's Dunstan now? He'll answer my questions, or leave this house! Go and fetch him at once!'

'Dunstan hasn't come home, sir. The horse was found dead, and nobody knows where Dunstan is.'

'Well, why did you let him have my money? Answer me!' said the Squire, staring angrily at Godfrey.

'Well, sir, I don't know,' replied Godfrey, hesitating. He was not good at lying, and was not prepared for his father's questions.

'You don't know?' the Squire repeated scornfully. 'Well, *I* know why. I think you've done something wrong, and you've bribed Dunstan to keep it a secret! That's it, isn't it?'

The Squire had made a very clever guess, and Godfrey's heart banged in sudden alarm. He was not ready to confess everything yet. 'Well, sir,' he said, trying to speak carelessly, 'it was just a little business between Dunstan and me. You wouldn't be interested in it, you know.'

'How old are you now? Twenty-six?' asked the Squire angrily. 'Old enough to look after your money and mine too! I've been much too generous to you boys, but I'm going to be harder on you all from now on. You've got a weak character, Godfrey, like your poor mother. I think you need a wife who knows what she wants, because you can't decide anything by yourself! When you were thinking of marrying Nancy Lammeter, I agreed, didn't I? Have you asked her or not? She hasn't refused to marry you, has she?'

'No, I haven't asked her,' said Godfrey, feeling very hot and uncomfortable, 'but I don't think she'll accept me.'

'Don't be stupid, Godfrey!' said the Squire with a scornful laugh. 'Any woman would want to marry into our family! Do you *want* to marry her?'

'There's no other woman I want to marry,' said Godfrey, avoiding his father's eyes.

'Well, then, let me speak to her father for you, since you aren't brave enough to do it yourself. She's a pretty girl, and intelligent.'

'No, sir, please don't say anything at the moment,' said Godfrey quickly. 'I must ask her myself.'

'Well, ask her then. When you marry her, you'll have to forget about horses and so on. It'll be good for you to do some serious work. You should get married soon.'

'Please don't try to hurry things, sir,' begged Godfrey.

'I'll do what I like,' said the Squire firmly. 'And if you don't do what I want, I'll disinherit you and you can leave the house. Now, if you know where Dunstan's hiding – I expect you do –

29

'You've got a weak character, Godfrey,' said the Squire angrily.

tell him he needn't come home. He'll pay for his own food from now on.'

'I don't know where he is, sir. Anyway, it's *you* who should tell him to leave home.'

'Don't argue with me, Godfrey,' said the Squire, turning back to his breakfast. 'Just go and tell the servants to get my horse ready.'

Godfrey left the room. He was relieved that his father had not discovered the whole truth. However, he was a little worried that the Squire would try to arrange his marriage with Nancy. While he was married to Molly, he could not marry Nancy, although it was his dearest wish. But as usual he was waiting and hoping for some unexpected change in his situation, which would save him from any unpleasantness.

— 5 —
Silas's neighbours

In the weeks following the robbery, the police tried hard to find the pedlar, because so many people suspected him of being the thief. But there was no sign of him in any of the towns and villages round Raveloe.

Nobody was surprised at Dunstan Cass's absence. Once before he had stayed away for six weeks and then come back. Nobody imagined he could have anything to do with the robbery. The villagers continued to discuss Silas and his lost gold, but they had no more explanations to offer.

Silas himself still had his loom and his work, so he went on weaving. But the only thing that had made his life worth living had gone, and now he had nothing to look forward to. A lifetime of empty evenings lay ahead of him. He did not enjoy thinking of the money he would earn, because it reminded him of the money he had lost. As he sat weaving, he sometimes used to moan quietly to himself. And in the evenings, as he sat alone in front of the fire, he used to put his head in his hands and moan again.

But this disaster had one good result. Little by little, Silas's neighbours realized it was wrong to be suspicious of him. He was just a poor, simple, harmless man, who needed their help. They showed their new opinion of him in many different ways. Some of the women, who were baking cakes and preparing meat for Christmas, brought him presents of food. Some of the men, who had nothing to give him, stopped him in the village to ask about his health, or visited him to discuss the robbery. They often finished their conversation by saying cheerfully, 'Now you're the same as the rest of us – we're poor too! Cheer up, Master Marner! If you get ill and can't work any more, the Squire'll give you food and your neighbours will take care of you.' This did not make Silas feel better, but he realized it was meant kindly.

Old Mr Macey, the church clerk, came to the cottage one day, to explain how his opinion of the weaver had changed.

'You see, Master Marner,' he said in his high old voice, 'I used to think you worked for the devil – you've always looked strange, you know. But now I'm sure you're not evil, just a little bit crazy. That's what I tell the neighbours.'

He stopped to give Silas time to reply, but the weaver did not speak. He was sitting with his head in his hands as usual. He knew that the old man was trying to be kind, but he was too miserable to show any interest.

'Come, Master Marner, what's your answer to that?' asked Mr Macey, a little impatiently.

'Oh,' said Silas, slowly lifting his head, 'thank you. Thank you for your kindness.'

'That's all right,' replied the old man, pleased. 'Now, you shouldn't sit here moaning, you know. Here's my advice to you. Ask Tookey in the village to make you a Sunday suit – I don't expect you've got one – and then you can come to church with your neighbours. It'll make you feel better. You're not an old man yet, although you look like one. How old were you when you came here first? Twenty-five?'

'I don't remember,' answered Silas, shaking his head.

That evening, Mr Macey told a number of villagers at the Rainbow, 'Poor Master Marner doesn't know how old he is! And I don't suppose he knows what day of the week it is! He really is a bit crazy.'

Another villager, Dolly Winthrop, was also worried about Silas's absence from church. She was a large, fresh-faced woman with a sweet, patient smile, who was always busy from early morning until late at night, and who went to church herself every Sunday. She believed in helping her neighbours, and if someone in Raveloe was ill or dying, Dolly was often asked to take care of the patient. This good, sensible woman decided that Silas needed her help. So one Sunday afternoon she took her son

Aaron, a pretty little boy of seven, to visit the weaver. As they came closer to the cottage, they heard the sound of the loom.

'Oh dear! Working on a Sunday! That's bad!' said Mrs Winthrop sadly. She had to knock loudly on the door before Silas heard. He said nothing, but opened the door to let them in, and Dolly sat down in an armchair.

'I was baking yesterday, Master Marner,' she said, 'and I've brought you some of my cakes. Here they are.'

'Thank you,' replied Silas, taking the little bag of cakes Dolly was holding out to him. Aaron was hiding behind his mother's chair, in childish fear of the weaver.

'You didn't hear the church bells this morning, perhaps, Master Marner?' Dolly asked gently. 'This cottage is a long way from the village.'

'Yes, I heard them,' answered Silas. For him Sunday bells did not mean anything. There had been no bells at the Light Street chapel.

'Oh!' said Dolly. 'But – but do you *have* to work on a Sunday? You could make Sunday different from the other days, you know, by washing yourself, and cooking a little piece of meat, and going to church. And Master Marner, Christmas Day will be here soon! If you put on your best clothes and go to church and see the flowers and hear the singing, you'll feel much better! You'll know there is Someone you can trust!'

Dolly did not usually talk so much, but the matter seemed extremely important to her.

'No, no,' Silas replied. 'I don't know anything about church. I've never been to church.'

'Never been!' repeated Dolly. 'Were there no churches in the town you were born in?'

'Oh yes,' said Silas, 'there were a lot of churches. It was a big town, you see. But I only ever went to chapel.'

Dolly did not understand this word, but was afraid of asking any more questions, in case 'chapel' meant something evil. After considering carefully for a moment, she said, 'Well, Master Marner, it's never too late to start going to church. It's very pleasant listening to the singing and the good words. If we go to church, then when trouble comes, Someone will take care of us. And if we do our best, then I believe Someone will help us when we need help.'

Dolly's explanation of her simple religion did not seem at all clear to Silas, but he did understand that she was asking him to go to church. He did not want to agree to that. Just then young Aaron came out from behind his mother's chair, and Silas offered him one of Dolly's cakes.

'Oh Aaron!' said his mother. 'You're always eating! No, don't give him any more, Master Marner. But he can sing a song for you. I'm sure you'll like it. It's a beautiful Christmas carol. Come, Aaron, let's hear it.'

Little Aaron stood up straight and sang his carol in a clear, sweet voice. Dolly listened with delight, hoping that the carol would help to persuade Silas to come to church.

'You see, Master Marner,' she said when Aaron had finished, '*that's* Christmas music. The Christmas Day service is wonderful, with all the voices and the music. I hope you'll be there with us. And remember, if you feel ill, I'll be happy to come and cook or

Little Aaron sang his carol in a clear, sweet voice.

clean for you. But I beg you, please stop weaving on Sundays. It's bad for soul and body, I'm sure. We must go now. Goodbye, Master Marner.'

'Thank you, and goodbye,' said Silas, as he opened the door for them. He could not help feeling relieved when she had gone. Now he could weave and moan as much as he liked.

Mr Macey and Dolly had tried hard to persuade Silas to go to church. But in the end he spent Christmas Day alone in his cottage, looking out at the cold grey sky. In the evening, snow began to fall, and he felt more distant and separate from his neighbours than ever. He sat in his robbed home, moaning miserably to himself, not noticing that his fire was no longer burning and that he was getting cold.

But in Raveloe the church bells were ringing and the church was fuller than all through the rest of the year. It was a special day for everybody, and after the service they all hurried home in the biting cold to eat and drink with their families.

At the Red House nobody spoke of Dunstan's absence. The village doctor, Dr Kimble, and his wife were guests there for Christmas lunch, and the day passed happily.

The servants, however, were already preparing for the New Year's Eve dance which Squire Cass gave every year. It was the best party of the year, and guests used to come from miles around. Godfrey was looking forward to this year's party more than usual. But he was still worried.

'What if Dunstan returns?' he thought. 'He'll tell the Squire about my secret marriage! And Molly's asking for more money! I'll have to sell something for cash. But on New Year's Eve, I can forget everything for an evening, and sit with Nancy, and look into her eyes, and dance with her . . .'

— 6 —
The New Year's Eve dance

On December 31st it was snowing and very cold. All day there were ladies and gentlemen arriving at the Red House.

Godfrey Cass was waiting at the door for the only guest he cared about, Nancy Lammeter. Finally she arrived, sitting behind her father on his horse, looking more beautiful than ever. Her lovely face blushed as she saw Godfrey come forward to lift her down from the horse. 'Why is he waiting for me?' she thought. 'I thought I made it clear to him that I'll never marry him. People say he leads a bad life, and I can't marry a man like that.'

But the Squire appeared just then, to welcome his guests, and in the excitement nobody noticed Nancy's pink face as Godfrey's strong arms lifted her down. She hurried into the house with the other ladies to change her clothes.

The house was full of servants running here and there. Mrs Kimble, who always helped the Squire arrange these parties, was giving orders in a loud voice. Cooks were preparing food in the kitchens, and there was already a wonderful smell of baking in the air.

Upstairs, the ladies were excitedly putting on their best dresses, while talking to each other all the time. Nancy met her aunt, Mrs Osgood, who introduced her to some visitors of hers. The Misses Gunn were two young ladies who were not beautiful, but dressed very fashionably.

Just then Nancy's older sister Priscilla arrived. She was a large, cheerful girl, with a round face and a nose pink with cold. As they were changing their clothes, Priscilla said to Mrs Osgood, 'Look at our dresses, aunt! Of course Nancy looks beautiful in hers, but this colour makes *me* look yellow! Nancy says we must wear the same dresses, because we're sisters, although I'm five years older! I'm ugly, I know I am. But I don't mind!' She turned to Mrs Osgood's two visitors. 'In my opinion the pretty girls are useful – I'm sure you agree – to catch the men. I don't think men are worth worrying about. Any woman with a good father and a good home had better stay single. That's what I'm going to do, anyway. We ugly girls don't need husbands!'

Mrs Osgood stood up and said quickly, 'My visitors and I should go downstairs now. Priscilla and Nancy, we'll see you later.' And the three ladies hurried out.

'Oh really, Priscilla!' cried Nancy, when they were alone. 'You never think before you speak! I'm sure the Misses Gunn thought you were very impolite! You almost told them they were ugly!'

'Did I?' asked Priscilla in surprise. 'Well, that's the way I am. I always tell the truth. But *I'm* the ugly one – just look at me!'

'Priscilla, you know I asked *you* to choose the dresses,' replied Nancy worriedly. 'I don't mind what colour I wear.'

'You look lovely in this colour, dear child! You know you

39

always have whatever you want in the end, although you never give orders or shout about it. I'm looking forward to seeing you married. It'll be fun watching you make your husband do exactly what you want.'

'Don't say that,' answered Nancy, blushing. 'You know I'm never going to get married.'

Priscilla laughed. '*I'm* the one who'll stay single. And if you don't like Godfrey Cass, well, there are plenty of other young men. Come, let's go downstairs now.'

Although Priscilla was right in saying she was not good-looking, she was very popular among her neighbours because she was so cheerful and sensible. And Nancy was not only considered to be the most beautiful girl in and around Raveloe, but also one of the most intelligent.

Seats at the dining-table had been kept for the Lammeter sisters. Priscilla was taken to sit between her father and the Squire. Nancy felt herself blushing again as Godfrey Cass came to lead her to a seat between himself and the vicar, Mr Crackenthorp. She knew that if she married Godfrey, she would one day be the most important woman in Raveloe, the Squire's wife. But she repeated firmly to herself that she could not marry a man of bad character.

As she sat down, the vicar, who was always polite to ladies, said with a smile, 'Ah, Miss Nancy, you're looking lovely this evening. Isn't she, Godfrey?'

Godfrey made no reply, and avoided looking at Nancy. There was too much he wanted to say to her. But the Squire, who always enjoyed his parties and was feeling extremely cheerful, was rather impatient with his son. He thought *he* had better speak, if Godfrey was too shy to do it himself.

'That's right,' the Squire said loudly. 'When I look at Miss Nancy here, I think she's more beautiful than any girl I've ever seen.'

While they were eating and drinking, people around the table were listening with interest to the Squire's words. 'Perhaps Godfrey will marry Nancy after all!' the vicar's wife whispered to Mrs Osgood. Mr Lammeter's back was very straight as he looked across the table at his daughter. He was a serious, careful gentleman, who considered the Lammeters a better family than the Casses. He had already decided that Godfrey must change his way of life before Nancy could possibly marry him.

Just then Dr Kimble called across the table, 'Miss Nancy, will you save a dance for me?'

'Come, come, Kimble,' said the Squire, 'let the young ones enjoy themselves. My son Godfrey'll be angry if you take Miss Nancy away. I expect he's asked her for the first dance already. Haven't you, Godfrey?'

Godfrey was feeling very uncomfortable by now. Turning to Nancy, he said as lightly as possible, 'I haven't asked her yet, but I hope she'll agree, if nobody's asked her . . .'

'No, I haven't accepted anyone else,' replied Nancy quietly with a blush.

'So will you please have the first dance with me?' asked Godfrey, beginning to feel better. She had not refused him!

'I will,' answered Nancy coldly. She was still sure she would not marry him, but she wanted to remain polite.

'Ah well, you're a lucky man, Godfrey,' said Dr Kimble with a laugh. 'I think I can hear the music starting now!'

The guests got up from the table in pairs and small groups, to move into the large hall, where the dancing was about to start. The small village band was already playing, as the Squire led the vicar's wife to the end of the hall to start the dance. They were followed by Godfrey and Nancy, and the other ladies and gentlemen.

As the dance went on, Godfrey felt happier and happier. Holding Nancy in his arms, he forgot all his problems. Suddenly the Squire's heavy foot stood on part of Nancy's dress, and some of the material was pulled away at the waist. Nancy asked Godfrey to take her to a quieter place, where she could repair the damage. He took her to a small room near the hall, hoping they would have a few private moments together. But Nancy sat down on the chair furthest away from him, and said coldly, 'Thank you, sir. You needn't stay. I'm very sorry about taking you away from the dance.'

'It's not very kind of you,' said Godfrey, moving close to her, 'to be sorry you've danced with me.'

'I didn't mean that!' replied Nancy, blushing prettily. 'Gentlemen have so many things to enjoy. I'm sure one dance can't matter very much.'

'You know that isn't true. You know one dance with you means more to me than anything else in the world.'

Nancy was a little surprised. Godfrey had not said anything like this to her for a long time. She replied firmly, 'I'm afraid I can't believe you, Mr Godfrey.'

Holding Nancy in his arms, Godfrey forgot all his problems.

'Nancy, if I changed my life, would you think better of me? Would you – like me, then?' Godfrey knew these were dangerous words, but the sudden chance of speaking to her alone made him say more than he had planned.

'I'd be glad to see a good change in anybody, sir.'

'You're very hard, Nancy,' said Godfrey bitterly. 'You could help me to be better. I'm very miserable – but *you* don't feel anything.'

'I think *people who behave badly* don't feel anything,' said Nancy sharply, forgetting to be cool and distant.

Godfrey was delighted. He wanted to make her argue with him, to show him that she cared about him. But just then Priscilla hurried in, saying, 'Dear child, let me look at your dress! I saw the Squire step on it during the dance.'

'I suppose I'd better go now,' Godfrey said disappointedly to Priscilla.

'It doesn't matter at all to me whether you go or stay,' said Priscilla impatiently, looking closely at the waist of Nancy's dress.

'Do *you* want me to go?' Godfrey asked Nancy.

'Do whatever you like,' replied Nancy, trying to sound cold again.

'Well, I want to stay,' answered Godfrey, and sat down. Tonight he wanted to enjoy being with Nancy for as long as possible, without thinking about what would happen tomorrow.

Silas finds his 'gold'

But while Godfrey Cass was managing to forget his problems by the lovely Nancy's side, his wife was walking with slow, uncertain steps along the snow-covered road to Raveloe. She was carrying her sleeping child in her arms.

For some time now she had planned to come to Raveloe on New Year's Eve. She knew that her husband would be at the centre of a happy, smiling group of friends, and she had chosen this moment to appear in front of all his family and guests at the Red House dance. 'I don't care if Godfrey is ashamed of me!' she thought bitterly. 'I want people to know we're married!' Sometimes she hated her husband, because he was still handsome, and had money, while she was no longer pretty, and very poor. She blamed him for her miserable life, but in her heart she knew she should blame her drinking. It had become a habit with her to spend most of the money Godfrey gave her on gin. She had a bottle in her pocket now, which she had lifted to her lips several times during her journey.

It was already seven o'clock in the evening, and there was a freezing wind. Molly did not know she was very near Raveloe. Her legs were tired and the gin was beginning to make her feel sleepy. She thought she would rest for a while, and, still holding her child, she lay down on the snow. She did not notice that the ground was cold.

In a few moments the child woke up, crying, 'Mummy!' But the mother did not seem to hear. Suddenly, as the child fell gently out of its mother's arms on to the soft snow, it noticed a bright, dancing light on the white ground. Interested, the child stood up to see where the brightness came from, and followed the light to an open door, the door of Silas Marner's cottage. The little one toddled right in through the door and sat down by the bright fire. After a few minutes the child felt pleasantly warm, and fell asleep.

But where was Silas while this was happening? In the evenings he sometimes used to open his door and look out. He had some idea that his money would come back, or that someone would come with information about the thief. Tonight was New Year's Eve, and the villagers had told him to stay awake until midnight, because it would bring him good luck if he saw the beginning of the new year. So tonight he was more restless than usual. He opened his door several times during the evening, and stared out, but he saw and heard nothing in the silent, freezing night. The last time, as he was standing at the door, he had one of his fits, and stood there completely unconscious, holding the door open.

When he became conscious again, he closed the door and turned back to the fire. But when his shortsighted eyes looked at the floor in front of the fire, he seemed to see gold there! Gold – his own gold – taken and then brought back to him in the same strange way! His heart beat excitedly, and for a few moments he was unable to move. At last he reached out his hand to touch the gold, but instead of hard, metal coins his fingers felt soft, warm curls.

With great surprise Silas fell on his knees to look at this

Instead of hard, metal coins his fingers felt soft, warm curls.

wonderful thing. It was a sleeping child. Was he dreaming? Could it be his little sister, who had died when he was a child himself? If it wasn't a dream, how had the child entered the cottage? But thinking of his sister made him remember the past, and his life at the Light Street chapel. He wondered if this child was some kind of message from his past, sent perhaps by the God he had once trusted.

Just then the child woke up, and began to cry. Silas held it in his arms, and spoke softly to quieten it. He remembered that he had made some porridge earlier, and gave a little to the child to eat. She stopped crying, and lifted her blue eyes with a smile to Silas's face as she ate. But then she pulled at her wet shoes, trying to take them off, and Silas suddenly realized she had come to the cottage through the snow. So he picked her up and went to the door. As he opened it and went out into the dark, the child cried 'Mummy!' and reached forward, almost jumping out of his arms. A few steps away, Silas found a young woman's body, half-covered with snow.

At the Red House, everybody was enjoying the party. Some people were still eating, while others were dancing or playing cards. Godfrey was looking forward to his next dance with Nancy. He was watching her dreamily across the room, when suddenly he saw something that made his lips go white and his whole body tremble. It was his own child, carried in Silas Marner's arms. The weaver had come straight into the hall, where the dancing was going on.

Several people turned to look at the strange figure in the

doorway. The Squire could not understand why Silas had come in uninvited. He stood up and asked angrily, 'Marner, what are you doing here?'

'I've come for the doctor,' replied Silas hurriedly. 'There's a woman – dead, I think – near my cottage.'

Godfrey had one great fear at that moment, that the woman was *not* dead. If she were his wife, and she were dead, he would be free to marry Nancy!

While the Squire was calling for Dr Kimble, the ladies came closer to look at the pretty child.

'Whose child is it?' one of them asked.

'I don't know,' replied Godfrey wildly. 'Some poor woman's – she's been found in the snow, I think.'

'You'd better leave the poor child here with us then, Master Marner,' offered Mrs Kimble kindly.

'No – I can't let it go,' said Silas unexpectedly. 'It's come to me – I don't know where from – I want to keep it!'

'Well!' said Mrs Kimble, surprised. 'A single man like you! Take care of a child! Well!' But the little one was holding on to Silas, and smiling up at him confidently.

Dr Kimble hurried into the hall. 'Where is this poor woman? Near the old quarry? Someone had better fetch Dolly Winthrop. I'll need her to help me.'

'I'll go!' cried Godfrey. He wanted to get away, before anyone noticed his white face and shaking hands, and he needed time to think. He ran out into the night.

When he and Dolly arrived at the quarry, the doctor had moved the woman into Silas's cottage, and Godfrey had to wait outside. He walked up and down in the snow, for what seemed like hours. He knew he should tell the truth about the woman and the child, but he could not make himself do what he knew was right. 'Is she dead?' the voice inside his head asked. 'If she is, I can marry Nancy. And then I'll be good, and have no more secrets. And I'll make sure the child is taken care of, of course.'

When Dr Kimble came out of the cottage, Godfrey tried to speak calmly. 'I thought I'd wait to see . . . ' he began.

'Oh, there was no need for you to come. Why didn't you send one of the men to fetch Dolly? The woman's dead, I'm afraid. She's very thin, and looks very poor. But she's got a wedding ring on. She'll be buried tomorrow.'

'I'll just have a look at her,' said Godfrey quickly. 'I think I saw a woman on the road yesterday with a child. Perhaps it was her.' And he ran into the cottage.

There on the bed was his unloved wife. He only looked at her for a moment, but for the rest of his life he never forgot her sad, tired face.

The weaver had come back with the doctor, and was sitting by the fire, with the child on his knees. The little one was awake, but her wide open blue eyes looked up into Godfrey's face without recognizing him at all. The father was glad of this, but also a little sad, especially when he saw the small hand pull lovingly at the weaver's grey hair.

'So, who's going to take care of the child?' Godfrey asked, pretending not to show much interest.

'*I* am,' replied Silas firmly. 'The mother's dead, and I suppose the child hasn't got a father. She's alone in the world, and so am I. My money's gone, I don't know where, and she's come, I don't know where from. I don't understand it at all, but I'm going to keep her.'

'Poor little thing!' said Godfrey. 'Let me give you something for her clothes.' He put his hand in his pocket and gave Silas some coins.

As he walked back to the Red House, he felt very relieved. Nobody would recognize his dead wife, and soon his secret would be buried with her. Now he could talk of love to Nancy. He could promise to be a good husband to her. Only Dunstan knew about the secret marriage, and perhaps Dunstan would never come home. 'What a good thing I didn't confess everything to the Squire!' he thought. 'Now I can make Nancy and myself happy. And the child? Well, it won't matter to her whether I'm her father or not.'

That week the dead woman was buried in Raveloe, and the child stayed at the weaver's cottage. The villagers were very surprised that Silas had decided to keep her, but they liked him for wanting to help an orphan. The women, especially, were very ready to give him useful advice on taking care of children.

Dolly Winthrop came every day to help Silas. 'It's no trouble,' she said. 'I get up early, so I've got plenty of time. And I can bring you some of Aaron's old baby clothes, so you won't need to spend a lot of money on the child. I can wash her, and give her food, and—'

'Ye–es,' said Silas, hesitating. He was looking a little jealously at the baby in Dolly's arms. 'That's very kind of you. But – but

*Silas's days and evenings were full, taking care of
a trusting, loving child.*

I want to do everything for her myself! I want her to be fond of *me*! She's *my* child!'

'Don't worry,' said Dolly gently, giving him the child. 'Look, she loves you the best. See, she's smiling at you!'

And so Silas learnt how to take care of the little girl. He called her Eppie, which had been his little sister's name. His life was quite different now. When he was working and living only for his gold, he had not been interested in the world outside his cottage, or the people he sometimes met. But now that he had another reason for living, he had to look outward. He spent hours in the fields with Eppie, happily rediscovering the plants he used to know so well. Together they visited his neighbours, who were always delighted to see him and his adopted child. His days and evenings were full, taking care of a trusting, loving child.

Godfrey Cass watched the little girl growing up with great interest. During Eppie's childhood he often gave money to Silas to spend on her, but was careful that nobody should suspect him of being her father. His life was also changing. There was a new firmness about him which everyone noticed. He was looking forward to marrying Nancy very soon. 'Nancy and I will have children!' he thought happily. 'But I won't forget that other child!'

— 8 —

Eppie has grown up

It was a bright autumn Sunday, sixteen years after Silas had found Eppie in his cottage. The Raveloe church bells were ringing, and people were coming out of church after the morning service. First came the new squire, Godfrey Cass, looking a little heavier now, but with a straight back and a firm step. On his arm was his wife Nancy, still a pretty woman. Just behind them came Mr Lammeter and Priscilla. They all went into the Red House.

'You and Priscilla will stay for tea, won't you?' Nancy asked her father.

'My dear, you must ask Priscilla,' replied Mr Lammeter with a smile. 'She manages me and the farm as well.'

'Well, it's better for your health if *I* manage everything, father,' said Priscilla. 'Then there's nothing for you to worry about. No, Nancy dear, we must go home now. But you and I can have a walk round the garden while the servants are getting the horses ready.'

When the sisters were alone in the garden, Priscilla said, 'My dear, I'm very glad you're going to have a dairy. Making your own butter will give you something to think about all the time. You'll never be sad when you've got a dairy.' And she put her arm through her sister's.

'Dear Priscilla,' said Nancy gratefully. 'I'm only ever sad when Godfrey is. I could be happy if *he* could accept our life as it is. But it's more difficult for a man.'

'Men!' cried Priscilla impatiently. 'They're always wanting something new! Never happy with what they've got! I'm glad I was too ugly to get married! I'm much happier with father!'

'Oh Priscilla,' said Nancy. 'Don't be angry with Godfrey – he's a very good husband. But of course he's disappointed that we haven't had children – he wanted them so much.'

'Well, father is waiting for me – I'd better go now. Goodbye, my dear.' And the sisters kissed goodbye.

When Priscilla and her father had left, Godfrey said, 'Nancy, I think I'll just go and look at some of the fields we're draining near the old quarry.'

'You'll be back by tea-time, dear?'

'Oh yes, I'll be back in an hour.'

This was a habit of Godfrey's on Sunday afternoons. He enjoyed walking round the fields that belonged to him now. So Nancy often had a quiet hour at about this time, which she spent reading, or sometimes just thinking.

She remembered all the little things that had happened to her, especially during her marriage, in the last fifteen years. The great sadness of her married life had been the death of her only baby. Like most women, she had looked forward to becoming a mother very much. But when the baby died soon after it was born, she made herself accept the fact. She did not allow herself to think about it, or to wish for anything different. Godfrey, however, had been terribly disappointed, especially when it seemed likely that Nancy could have no more children.

Nancy's religion was extremely important to her. She firmly believed that people should accept whatever happened to them in life, because it was God who decided everything. But she understood how difficult it was for Godfrey to accept that their marriage would be childless. 'Was I right,' she wondered for the hundredth time, 'to refuse him, when he said we should adopt a child? I believe that if God hasn't given us a child, it's because God doesn't want us to have one. I'm sure I'm right. But poor Godfrey! It's worse for him than for me. I've got him, and the house, and now the dairy to think about. But although he's always good to me, I know he's unhappy – he wants children so much!'

From the first moment Godfrey had spoken of adopting a child, he had mentioned Eppie's name. She had always been the child he wanted to adopt. He had no idea that Silas would rather die than lose Eppie, and he imagined that the weaver would be glad if the child were adopted by the Cass family. 'After all, the girl will have a much better life with us,' he told himself. 'I can't be really happy if we don't have a child. And I can never tell Nancy the truth about Eppie – I'm afraid she'll hate me for it.'

While Nancy was sitting quietly in the Red House, thinking about her husband, Silas and Eppie were sitting outside their cottage near the quarry. They had been to church too, which they did every week, like the Casses and most of the villagers. Silas had started taking Eppie to church when she was very young, because Dolly Winthrop had persuaded him that every child should have some religious training. Because of Eppie, Silas was completely accepted in Raveloe now. Nobody thought he was strange any more; in fact, he was almost a popular figure in the village.

Silas and Eppie were sitting outside their cottage.

He was older now, and could not work as hard as he used to. Recently, as he had more time to think, he had begun to remember the past, and his old friends at the Light Street chapel. He realized how his once lonely life had changed since Eppie had come to him. Now he had friends, and trusted people, and was happy. And he began to see that the God in the Raveloe church was the same God he had been so angry with, the last time he had been to the chapel. It seemed to him that there had been some mistake in his past, which had thrown a dark shadow over his early life. Perhaps now he would never know whether Mr Paston, the chapel minister, still thought he was guilty of stealing. And he would never discover why the drawing of the lots had seemed to prove his guilt. 'But there must be a God of goodness in this world,' he thought, 'because He sent Eppie to me. I must just trust, and believe that He is right.'

He had told Eppie how her mother had died in the snow, and he had given her the dead woman's wedding ring. Eppie was not at all interested in who her real father was, as she thought she had the best father in the world already. At the moment she was sitting close to Silas outside their door in the sunshine. Neither of them had spoken for a while.

'Father,' she said gently, 'if I get married, do you think I should wear my mother's ring?'

'Oh, Eppie!' said Silas, surprised. 'Are you thinking of getting married, then?'

'Well, Aaron was talking to me about it,' replied Eppie, blushing. 'You know he's nearly twenty-four now, and is earning good money, and he'd like to marry soon.'

'And who would he like to marry?' asked Silas with rather a sad smile.

'Why, me, of course, daddy!' said Eppie, laughing and kissing her father. 'He won't want to marry anyone else!'

'And you'd like to marry him, would you?' asked Silas.

'Yes, one day. I don't know when. Aaron says everyone's married some time. But I told him that's not true, because *you* haven't ever been married, have you, daddy?'

'No, child,' said Silas. 'I was a lonely man before you were sent to me.'

'But you'll never be lonely again, father,' said Eppie lovingly. 'That's what Aaron said. He doesn't want to take me away from you. He wants us all to live together, and he'll do all the work, and you needn't work at all, father. He'll be like a son to you.'

'Well, my child, you're young to be married,' said Silas. 'But he's a good young man. We'll ask his mother what we should do. She always gives us good advice. You see, Eppie, I'm getting older, and I'd like to think of you with a strong young husband to take care of you for the rest of your life. Yes, we'll ask Dolly Winthrop for her opinion.'

— 9 —
Godfrey confesses at last

At the Red House Nancy was waiting patiently for Godfrey to come home to tea. Suddenly one of the servants ran into the sitting-room, crying excitedly, 'Madam, there are lots of people in the street! They're all running the same way, towards the quarry! Perhaps there's been an accident!'

'Jane, don't get so excited,' replied Nancy calmly. 'I expect it's nothing serious. Go and get the tea ready. Mr Godfrey will be back soon.' But secretly she was saying to herself, 'I hope nothing's happened to Godfrey!'

So when he came into the room, a few minutes later, she was very relieved. 'My dear, I'm so thankful you've come,' she said, going towards him. 'I was beginning to think—'

She stopped suddenly when she saw Godfrey's shaking hands and white face. She put her hand on his arm, but he did not seem to notice, and threw himself into a chair.

'Sit down – Nancy,' he said with difficulty. 'I came back as soon as I could, to prevent anyone telling you except me. It's terrible news for me, but I'm more worried about how *you* will feel about it.'

'It isn't father or Priscilla?' said Nancy, trying to control her trembling lips.

'No, it's nobody living,' said Godfrey. 'It's Dunstan, my brother, who left home sixteen years ago and never came back. We've found him . . . found his body – all that's left of it – in the old quarry.'

Nancy felt calmer now. *That* was not terrible news.

'You know the men have been draining our fields near the quarry. Well, as a result, the quarry has suddenly gone dry, and we've found him lying at the bottom. We know it's him because he's wearing his watch and his rings.'

Godfrey paused. It was not easy to say what came next.

'Do you think he drowned himself?' asked Nancy, wondering why her husband was so shaken by the death of a brother he had never loved.

'No, he fell in,' replied Godfrey in a low voice. 'Dunstan was the man who robbed Silas Marner. The bags of gold were found with his body.'

'Oh Godfrey! I *am* sorry!' said Nancy. She understood how ashamed her husband must be. The Casses were so proud of their family name.

'I had to tell you. I couldn't keep it from you,' Godfrey continued, and then stopped, looking at the ground for two long minutes. Nancy knew that he had something more to say. Finally Godfrey lifted his eyes to her face, and said, 'Everybody's secrets are discovered sooner or later, Nancy. I've lived with a secret ever since I married you, but I'm going to confess it now. I don't want you to discover it from someone else, or hear about it when I'm dead. I was weak and hesitating when I was younger – I'm going to be firm with myself now.'

Nancy could not speak. She stared at her husband in horror. What secret could he possibly have from her?

'Nancy,' said Godfrey slowly, 'when I married you, I hid something from you – I was wrong not to tell you. That woman Silas Marner found dead in the snow – Eppie's mother – that poor woman – was my wife. Eppie is my child.'

He paused, looking worriedly at Nancy. But she sat quite still, although her face looked rather white.

'Perhaps you won't be able to love me any more,' he said, his voice trembling a little.

'The bags of gold were found with Dunstan's body.'

She was silent.

'I was wrong, I know I was wrong to marry Molly and then to keep it a secret. But I loved you, Nancy, I only ever wanted to marry you.'

Still Nancy was silent, looking down at her hands. And Godfrey almost expected her to get up and say she would leave him and go to live with her father and sister. She was so religious, and so firm in her ideas of right and wrong!

But at last she lifted her eyes to his and spoke. She did not sound angry, but only sad. 'Oh Godfrey, why didn't you tell me this long ago? I didn't know Eppie was yours and so I refused to adopt her. Of course I'd accept *your child* into our home! But – oh, Godfrey – how sad to think we've spent all these years with no children! Why didn't you confess the truth before we married? We could be so happy now, with a beautiful daughter, who would love me as her mother!' Tears were running down Nancy's face.

'But Nancy,' cried Godfrey, bitterly angry with himself, 'I couldn't tell you everything! I was in danger of losing you if I told you the truth!'

'I don't know about that, Godfrey. I certainly never wanted to marry anyone else. But it wasn't worth doing wrong just so that you could marry me. And our marriage hasn't been as happy for you as you thought it would be.' There was a sad smile on Nancy's face as she said the last words.

'Can you ever forgive me for what I've done, Nancy?'

'You have only hurt *me* a little, Godfrey, and you've been a good husband to me for fifteen years. But it's the other woman who you've hurt the most, and I don't see how you can put that right.'

'But we can take Eppie into our home now,' said Godfrey.

'It'll be different now that she's grown up,' said Nancy, shaking her head sadly. 'It'll be more difficult for her to get used to us. But it's our duty to take care of your child, and I'll ask God to make her love me.'

'Then we'll go to the weaver's cottage tonight,' said Godfrey, 'and talk to Marner and Eppie about it.'

— 10 —
Eppie has to decide

That evening Silas was resting in his chair near the fire, after the excitement of the day. Eppie was sitting close to him, holding both his hands, and on the table was Silas's lost gold. He had put the coins in piles, as he used to.

'You see, that's all I ever did in the long evenings before you came to me,' he was telling Eppie, 'just count my gold. I was only half alive in those days. What a good thing the money was taken away from me! I was killing myself with working all day, and counting money half the night. It wasn't a healthy life. And when you came, with your yellow curls, I thought *you* were the gold. And then, when I began to love you, I didn't want my gold any more.' He stopped talking for a moment and looked at the money. 'The gold doesn't mean anything to me now. But perhaps, if I ever lost you, Eppie, if you ever went away from me,

I'd need my gold again. I'd feel lonely then, and I'd think God had forgotten me, and perhaps I'd go back to my bad old habits.'

There were tears in Eppie's beautiful eyes, but she did not have time to answer Silas, as just then there was a knock on the door. When she opened it, Mr and Mrs Godfrey Cass came in.

'Good evening, my dear,' said Nancy, taking Eppie's hand gently. 'We're sorry to come so late.'

'Well, Marner,' said Godfrey, as he and Nancy sat down, 'I'm glad you've got your money back, and I'm very sorry it was one of my family who stole it from you. Whatever I can do for you, I will, to repay what I owe you – and I owe you a lot, Marner.'

Silas was always uncomfortable with important people like the young Squire. 'You don't owe me anything, sir. You've already been very kind to me. And that money on the table is more than most working people can save in their whole life. Eppie and I don't need very much.'

Godfrey was impatient to explain why they had come. 'Yes, you've done well these last sixteen years, Marner, taking care of Eppie here. She looks pretty and healthy, but not very strong. Don't you think she should be a lady, not a working woman? Now Mrs Cass and I, you know, have no children, and we'd like to adopt a daughter to live with us in our beautiful home and enjoy all the good things we're used to. In fact, we'd like to have Eppie. I'm sure you'd be glad to see her become a lady, and of course we'd make sure *you* have everything you need. And Eppie will come to see you very often, I expect.'

Godfrey did not find it easy to say what he felt, and as a result his words were not chosen sensitively. Silas was hurt, and afraid. His whole body trembled as he said quietly to Eppie after a moment, 'I won't stand in your way, my child. Thank Mr and Mrs Cass. It's very kind of them.'

Eppie stepped forward. She was blushing, but held her head high. 'Thank you, sir and madam. But I can't leave my father. And I don't want to be a lady, thank you.' She went back to Silas's chair, and put an arm round his neck, brushing the tears from her eyes.

Godfrey was extremely annoyed. He wanted to do what he thought was his duty. And adopting Eppie would make him feel much less guilty about his past. 'But, Eppie, you *must* agree,' he cried. '*You are my daughter!* Marner, Eppie's my own child. Her mother was my wife.'

Eppie's face went white. Silas, who had been relieved by hearing Eppie's answer to Godfrey, now felt angry. 'Then, sir,' he answered bitterly, 'why didn't you confess this sixteen years ago, before I began to love her? Why do you come to take her away now, when it's like taking the heart out of my body? God gave her to me because you turned your back on her! And He considers her mine!'

'I know I was wrong, and I'm sorry,' said Godfrey. 'But be sensible, Marner! She'll be very near you and will often come to see you. She'll feel just the same towards you.'

'Just the same?' said Silas more bitterly than ever. 'How *can* she feel the same? We're used to spending all our time together! We need each other!'

Godfrey thought the weaver was being very selfish. 'I think,

'Why do you come to take Eppie away now, when it's like
taking the heart out of my body?' said Silas bitterly.

Marner,' he said firmly, 'that you should consider what's best for Eppie. You shouldn't stand in her way, when she could have a better life. I'm sorry, but I think it's my duty to take care of my own daughter.'

Silas was silent for a moment. He was worried that perhaps Godfrey was right, and that it was selfish of him to keep Eppie. At last he made himself bring out the difficult words. 'All right. I'll say no more. Speak to the child. I won't prevent her from going.'

Godfrey and Nancy were relieved to hear this, and thought that Eppie would now agree. 'Eppie, my dear,' said Godfrey, 'although I haven't been a good father to you so far, I want to do my best for you now. And my wife will be the best of mothers to you.'

'I've always wanted a daughter, my dear,' added Nancy in her gentle voice.

But Eppie did not come forward this time. She stood by Silas's side, holding his hand in hers, and spoke almost coldly. 'Thank you, sir and madam, for your kind offer. But I wouldn't be happy if I left father. He'd have nobody if I weren't here. Nobody shall ever come between him and me!'

'But you must make sure, Eppie,' said Silas worriedly, 'that you won't be sorry, if you decide to stay with poor people. You could have a much better life at the Red House.'

'I'll never be sorry, father,' said Eppie firmly. 'I don't want to be rich, if I can't live with the people I know and love.'

Nancy thought she could help to persuade Eppie. 'What you say is natural, my dear child,' she said kindly. 'But there's a duty you owe to your lawful father. If he opens his home to you, you shouldn't turn your back on him.'

'But I can't think of any home except this one!' cried Eppie, tears running down her face. 'I've only ever known one father! And I've promised to marry a working man, who'll live with us, and help me take care of father!'

Godfrey looked at Nancy. 'Let's go,' he said to her bitterly, in a low voice.

'We won't talk of this any more,' said Nancy, getting up. 'We just want the best for you, Eppie my dear, and you too, Marner. Good night.'

Nancy and Godfrey left the cottage and walked home in the moonlight. When they reached home, Godfrey dropped into a chair. Nancy stood near him, waiting for him to speak. After a few moments he looked up at her, and took her hand.

'That's ended!' he said sadly.

She kissed him and then said, 'Yes, I'm afraid we can't hope to adopt her, if she doesn't want to come to us.'

'No,' said Godfrey, 'it's too late now. I made mistakes in the past, and I can't put them right. I wanted to be childless once, Nancy, and now I'll always be childless.'

He thought for a moment, and then spoke in a softer voice. 'But I've got *you*, Nancy, and yet I've been wanting something different all the time. Perhaps from now on I'll be able to accept our life better, and we'll be happier.'

The following spring, there was a wedding in Raveloe. The sun shone warmly as Eppie walked through the village towards the church, with Silas, Aaron and Dolly. Eppie was wearing the beautiful white wedding dress she had always dreamed of, which Nancy Cass had bought for her. She was walking arm in arm with her father, Silas.

'I promise nothing will change when I'm married, father,' she whispered to him as they entered the church. 'You know I'll never leave you.'

There was quite a crowd of villagers outside the church to see the wedding. Just then Miss Priscilla Lammeter and her father drove into the village.

'Look, father!' cried Priscilla. 'How lucky! We're in time to see the weaver's daughter getting married! Doesn't she look lovely? I'm sorry Nancy couldn't find a pretty little orphan girl like that to take care of.'

'Yes, my dear,' agreed Mr Lammeter. 'Now that we're all getting older, it would be good to have a young one in the family. Unfortunately, it's too late now.'

They went into the Red House, where Nancy was waiting for them. They had come to spend the day with her, because Godfrey was away on business and she would perhaps be lonely without him. The Casses were not going to Eppie's wedding.

When the little wedding group came out of the church, the villagers and Silas's family all went to the Rainbow. There a wonderful wedding lunch was waiting for them, which had been ordered and paid for by Godfrey Cass.

'It's very generous of the young Squire to pay for all this,' said the landlord as he refilled the beer glasses.

'Well, what would you expect?' replied old Mr Macey

'Look! We're in time to see the weaver's daughter getting married!'

sharply. 'Remember, it was his own brother who stole the weaver's gold! And Mr Godfrey has always helped Master Marner, with furniture and clothes and so on, since young Eppie came to the cottage. Well, it's only right to help a man like Master Marner. And I'd like you all to remember – I was the first to tell you I thought Master Marner was harmless – and I was right! Now let's drink to the health of the happy young couple!' And the villagers lifted their glasses and cried, 'To Eppie and Aaron!'

When the meal was over and the guests had begun to return to their homes, Silas, Eppie and her new husband walked slowly back to their cottage by the quarry. It had been enlarged by Godfrey Cass's workmen, and was looking lovely in the late afternoon sunshine.

'Oh father,' said Eppie. 'What a pretty home ours is! I think nobody could be happier than we are!'

GLOSSARY

absence being away or absent

adopt to take another person's child into your family to
    become your own child

bitter feeling disappointed and angry

blush *(v and n)* to become red in the face when ashamed or shy

butcher someone whose job is to cut and sell meat

carol a song usually sung at Christmas

chapel a room or building used for religious meetings

cheerful feeling happy or causing other people to feel happy

confess to tell the truth about something you have done wrong

cottage a small, simple house, usually in the country

curl *(n)* a piece of hair that grows round and round, in rings

dairy a place where milk is kept and butter, cheese, etc. are made

devil the enemy of God, or a bad, evil person

drain *(v)* to make land dryer by causing the water to run off it

draw lots to decide something by taking pieces of paper (with
    numbers or writing on them) out of a covered box

duty something you feel you have to do because it is right

engaged having promised to marry someone

evil *(adj and n)* very bad or wrong

farrier someone who puts new shoes on horses

firm *(adj)* strong and determined

fit *(n)* a sudden illness, when a person is unconscious for a time

forgive to say or show that you are not angry with someone

gamble *(v)* to play games of chance (e.g. card games) for money

gentleman a man of good family, usually rich

gin a strong, colourless alcoholic drink

guilt a feeling that you have done wrong

hunt *(v and n)* to chase and kill wild animals
landlord a man who controls a public house
linen a special kind of cloth (more like cotton than wool)
loom a machine for weaving cloth
Master a title used for an experienced workman (not used now)
minister a religious leader (e.g. a chapel minister)
moan *(v)* to make a long, sad sound that shows you are unhappy
New Year's Eve 31st December, the day before the New Year
orphan a child whose parents are dead
pedlar a person who travels from place to place selling things
pile *(n)* a lot of things on top of one another
poacher a person who catches animals from other people's land
porridge a cooked breakfast cereal, eaten hot
power being able to do something (sometimes unusual things)
quarry a place where stone, sand, etc. are taken out of the
   ground
relieved glad that a problem has gone away
religion *(adj* **religious***)* a belief in a god or gods, and the different
   ways of showing the belief
scornful feeling strongly that something or someone is worthless
service a religious meeting in a church or chapel
shortsighted being able to see clearly only things that are close
soul the part of us that some people believe does not die
Squire the title for the most important gentleman or landowner
   in a country area (not used now)
suspicious not believing or trusting someone
toddle (of a very young child) to walk with short uncertain steps
trust *(v and n)* to feel sure that someone is good, right, honest, etc.
vicar a priest in the Church of England
weak not strong, easily persuaded
weave to make cloth using a loom

Silas Marner

ACTIVITIES

Before Reading

1 Read the story introduction on the first page of the book, and the back cover. What do you know now about Silas Marner and the people of Raveloe? Circle Y (Yes) or N (No) for each of these sentences.

1 Everyone in Raveloe lives in a small cottage. Y/N
2 Silas Marner lives only for his gold. Y/N
3 Silas lives with his parents. Y/N
4 All the villagers work on Sundays. Y/N
5 Silas earns his gold by weaving linen. Y/N

2 'The Squire's two sons share a secret.' Can you guess what their secret is? Choose one of these ideas.

1 They borrowed money, which they have to return soon.
2 They have both told lies to their father.
3 They are both in love with the same woman.
4 One of them has made a foolish marriage.
5 One of them has committed a crime.

3 What kind of 'comfort' would help Silas to go on living, if his gold were stolen? Choose one of these ideas.

1 Finding the thief and seeing him punished.
2 Finding someone to love, to replace his gold.
3 Earning more gold through his work.

While Reading

Read Chapters 1 and 2, and answer these questions.

1 Why were country people suspicious of linen-weavers?
2 How long had Silas Marner lived in Raveloe?
3 When Silas lived in the town, why did the chapel minister believe that Silas had been chosen by God?
4 What was Silas accused of?
5 What did Silas think had really happened?
6 Why did Silas shut himself away in his cottage at Raveloe?
7 What did Silas do every evening in his cottage?
8 What were Godfrey and Dunstan Cass arguing about?
9 What was the secret that Dunstan knew about Godfrey?
10 Why was Godfrey afraid to confess the truth to his father?
11 How did Dunstan suggest getting the money?
12 What happened at the hunt?
13 What did Dunstan do on the way home?

Before you read Chapter 3 (*Where is Silas's gold?*), can you guess what happens? Choose Y (yes) or N (no) for each idea.

1 Dunstan disappears and is never seen alive again. Y/N
2 Dunstan shares the gold with Godfrey. Y/N
3 Silas goes to the village and asks for help. Y/N
4 Most people think that a stranger has stolen the gold. Y/N
5 Silas tell nobody about the loss of his gold. Y/N

Read Chapters 3 to 5. Are these sentences true (T) or false (F)? Rewrite the false sentences with the correct information.

1 Silas suspected Jem Rodney of stealing his gold.
2 The villagers also thought that Jem was the thief.
3 Godfrey cared more about Dunstan than about his horse.
4 Godfrey told the Squire the truth about Fowler's money.
5 The Squire did not want Godfrey to marry Nancy.
6 After the robbery the villagers' opinion of Silas changed.
7 Dolly Winthrop tried to persuade Silas to go to church.
8 Dolly understood that a chapel was a kind of church.
9 Silas no longer felt miserable about his stolen gold.

Before you read Chapters 6 and 7, can you guess what happens on New Year's Eve?

1 Will Dunstan come home, after spending all Silas's gold?
2 Will the Squire learn about Godfrey's secret marriage?
3 Will Godfrey ask Nancy to marry him at the dance?
4 Will he confess to Nancy that he is already married?
5 Will Godfrey's wife Molly come to Raveloe?
6 Will Silas find his gold again?

Read Chapters 6 and 7. Who said or thought this? Who were they talking or thinking about?

1 'I expect he's asked her for the first dance already.'
2 'You could help me to be better.'
3 'I think people who behave badly don't feel anything.'
4 'There's a woman – dead, I think – near my cottage.'

5 'A single man like you! Take care of a child! Well!'

6 'She's very thin, and looks very poor.'

7 'I don't understand it at all, but I'm going to keep her.'

8 'It won't matter to her whether I'm her father or not.'

9 'Look, she loves you the best. See, she's smiling at you!'

10 'But I won't forget that other child!'

Read Chapters 8 and 9. Choose the best question-word for these questions, and then answer them.

What / Why

1 . . . was the great sadness of Nancy's married life?

2 . . . had Nancy refused to adopt a child?

3 . . . had Godfrey wanted to adopt Eppie?

4 . . . wasn't Eppie interested in who her real father was?

5 . . . did Silas think of Eppie's marriage plans?

6 . . . was found in the quarry?

7 . . . did Godfrey finally confess his secret to Nancy?

8 . . . was Nancy so sad when she learnt the truth?

9 . . . did Godfrey and Nancy decide to do?

Before you read Chapter 10 (*Eppie has to decide*), can you guess how the story will end?

1 What will Eppie decide, and why?

2 Will Silas be glad to have Eppie adopted by the Casses?

3 Will Eppie be happier with her real father, or with Silas?

4 Whatever Eppie decides, will she change her mind later?

5 Will Eppie marry Aaron Winthrop?

After Reading

1 **Here are some of the villagers talking. Who are they talking about, and what has just happened in the story?**

   1 'We know she was married, don't we? She had a wedding
     ring on. But who she was, and where she was going, we'll
     never know. Poor thing!'

   2 'His face went as white as a sheet! It happened a long time
     ago, of course, but still – it's awful to learn that one of
     your own family was a thief.'

   3 'It's strange, isn't it? She paid for the dress, and he paid for
     the lunch, but neither of them were at the church. I
     wonder why not?'

   4 'She's been to see him, told him all about the singing in
     church. Even got her boy to sing to him. But he just wasn't
     interested, she says.'

   5 'At first we thought it was a ghost! There he was, in the
     doorway, with a white face and those strange staring eyes.
     Just like a madman, with no coat on, and dripping wet!'

   6 'Did you see them last Sunday? You could see she'd been
     crying. And he looked miserable too, didn't he? Must be a
     terrible disappointment to both of them. But they're still
     young – let's hope there'll be another on the way soon!'

2 **When Silas told Eppie how he had found and adopted her (see page 58), what did Eppie say? Complete her side of the conversation.**

SILAS: Now, Eppie, I've got something to give you.

EPPIE: _____

SILAS: That's right, it's a wedding ring, and it used to belong to your mother. So it's yours now.

EPPIE: _____

SILAS: Poor woman! She died in the snow on New Year's Eve, when you were about two years old.

EPPIE: _____

SILAS: She wasn't in good health, my dear, and she'd got very tired and cold, walking in the snow.

EPPIE: _____

SILAS: Oh, you were with her, Eppie. When she fell down, you toddled into my cottage, and fell asleep in front of my fire. And that's how I found you!

EPPIE: _____

SILAS: Well, no, Eppie, not your real father. I adopted you, you see, and you call me father, but—

EPPIE: _____

SILAS: I'm afraid nobody knows, my dear. Does that make you sad?

EPPIE: _____

SILAS: And I think you're the best daughter in the world, Eppie! My life has been so different since I found you – I hope nobody will ever take you away from me!

3 **Perhaps Nancy wrote her diary on the day when she and Godfrey visited Silas's cottage to ask Eppie to live with them. Choose one suitable word to fill each gap.**

I still find it _____ to believe what has _____! To learn that Godfrey _____ a daughter, after all _____ years! But I thought it _____ too much to hope _____. Poor Godfrey is very _____. He was sure the _____ would want Eppie to _____ to us. He just _____ realize it was all _____ late. Of course, it's _____ that Eppie feels more _____ the man who's looked _____ her all these years _____ for the man who's _____ recognized her as his _____. If only he'd confessed _____ to me when we _____, or at least not _____ it a secret for _____ long. And now I _____ get used to being _____ until I die, with _____ to care for and _____, and no grandchildren to _____ forward to. I would _____ so happy, with a _____ like Eppie at my _____! But I'm fortunate to _____ a very kind husband _____ loves me. Perhaps our _____ will be happier in _____, now that we understand _____ other better, and there _____ no more secrets between _____.

4 **Even in a quiet village like Raveloe, exciting things happen sometimes. Here are some headlines from a local newspaper. Use the notes below to write a short paragraph to go with each headline.**

ROBBERY AT RAVELOE
- two bags of gold / floorboards / cottage / Raveloe
- belong / weaver / Silas Marner
- thief / unknown / suspicious / pedlar / visit / recently

WOMAN DEAD IN SNOW

- New Year's Eve / woman /dead / snow / Raveloe
- name / unknown / wedding ring / who / husband
- two-year-old child / safe and well
- local weaver / found child / plan / adopt

BODY FOUND IN QUARRY

- yesterday / work / drain / Squire's fields / Raveloe / body / young man / old quarry
- recognize / Dunstan Cass / brother / Squire Cass / watch and rings / found / body
- two bags of gold / weaver / cottage / sixteen years ago
- clear / Dunstan Cass / disappeared / thief

WEDDING AT RAVELOE

- last week / Eppie / weaver / Aaron Winthrop / church
- Nancy Cass / wedding dress / the Squire / wedding lunch
- young couple / father / cottage

5 **What is *your* opinion about these ideas from the story?**

1 EPPIE: 'I don't want to be rich, if I can't live with the people I know and love.' Is Eppie right? Is money ever more important than happiness? If so, when?

2 NANCY: 'There's a duty you owe to your lawful father.' Is Nancy right? Should you always do what your parents want? Why, or why not?

3 GODFREY: 'I made mistakes in the past, and I can't put them right.' Is Godfrey right? How can people put right mistakes they have made?

ABOUT THE AUTHOR

Mary Ann (or Marian) Evans was born in 1819 on a farm near Coventry, in the English Midlands. At school and afterwards, she studied several languages and read widely, and all her life she had a deep interest in religious ideas of love and duty. She wrote articles about these ideas, and published translations from German religious works. In 1851 she moved to London, where she fell in love with the writer George Henry Lewes. They did not marry (Lewes was already married and unable to divorce), but lived together happily until Lewes's death in 1878.

Encouraged by Lewes, Marian began writing fiction, using the name George Eliot, as women novelists were often not taken seriously at the time. Her first work, *Scenes of Clerical Life* (1858), received warm praise. She went on to write seven more novels, which included *The Mill on the Floss* (1860), *Silas Marner* (1861), described by George Eliot as 'a story of old-fashioned village life', and *Middlemarch* (1871–2). The novels brought her fame and success, and admirers as different as Henry James and Queen Victoria. She died in 1880, only a few months after marrying John Walter Cross, an old friend.

George Eliot is one of the great English novelists. She was highly educated and extremely intelligent (many people found her conversation alarmingly clever), and her deep understanding of people and the society of her day widened the horizons of the novel as an art form. *Middlemarch* – made into a popular television series in the 1990s – is probably her greatest work, and was said by Virginia Woolf, another famous novelist, to be 'one of the few English novels written for grown-up people'.

OXFORD BOOKWORMS LIBRARY

Classics • Crime & Mystery • Factfiles • Fantasy & Horror
Human Interest • Playscripts • Thriller & Adventure
True Stories • World Stories

The OXFORD BOOKWORMS LIBRARY provides enjoyable reading in English, with a wide range of classic and modern fiction, non-fiction, and plays. It includes original and adapted texts in seven carefully graded language stages, which take learners from beginner to advanced level. An overview is given on the next pages.

All Stage 1 titles are available as audio recordings, as well as over eighty other titles from Starter to Stage 6. All Starters and many titles at Stages 1 to 4 are specially recommended for younger learners. Every Bookworm is illustrated, and Starters and Factfiles have full-colour illustrations.

The OXFORD BOOKWORMS LIBRARY also offers extensive support. Each book contains an introduction to the story, notes about the author, a glossary, and activities. Additional resources include tests and worksheets, and answers for these and for the activities in the books. There is advice on running a class library, using audio recordings, and the many ways of using Oxford Bookworms in reading programmes. Resource materials are available on the website <www.oup.com/elt/bookworms>.

The *Oxford Bookworms Collection* is a series for advanced learners. It consists of volumes of short stories by well-known authors, both classic and modern. Texts are not abridged or adapted in any way, but carefully selected to be accessible to the advanced student.

You can find details and a full list of titles in the *Oxford Bookworms Library Catalogue* and *Oxford English Language Teaching Catalogues*, and on the website <www.oup.com/elt/bookworms>.

THE OXFORD BOOKWORMS LIBRARY
GRADING AND SAMPLE EXTRACTS

STARTER • 250 HEADWORDS

present simple – present continuous – imperative –
can/cannot, must – *going to* (future) – simple gerunds ...

Her phone is ringing – but where is it?

Sally gets out of bed and looks in her bag. No phone. She looks under the bed. No phone. Then she looks behind the door. There is her phone. Sally picks up her phone and answers it. ***Sally's Phone***

STAGE 1 • 400 HEADWORDS

... past simple – coordination with *and*, *but*, *or* –
subordination with *before*, *after*, *when*, *because*, *so* ...

I knew him in Persia. He was a famous builder and I worked with him there. For a time I was his friend, but not for long. When he came to Paris, I came after him – I wanted to watch him. He was a very clever, very dangerous man. ***The Phantom of the Opera***

STAGE 2 • 700 HEADWORDS

... present perfect – *will* (future) – *(don't) have to, must not, could* –
comparison of adjectives – simple *if* clauses – past continuous –
tag questions – *ask/tell* + infinitive ...

While I was writing these words in my diary, I decided what to do. I must try to escape. I shall try to get down the wall outside. The window is high above the ground, but I have to try. I shall take some of the gold with me – if I escape, perhaps it will be helpful later. ***Dracula***

... *should, may* – present perfect continuous – *used to* – past perfect –
causative – relative clauses – indirect statements ...

Of course, it was most important that no one should see
Colin, Mary, or Dickon entering the secret garden. So Colin
gave orders to the gardeners that they must all keep away
from that part of the garden in future. *The Secret Garden*

STAGE 4 • 1400 HEADWORDS

... past perfect continuous – passive (simple forms) –
would conditional clauses – indirect questions –
relatives with *where/when* – gerunds after prepositions/phrases ...

I was glad. Now Hyde could not show his face to the world
again. If he did, every honest man in London would be proud
to report him to the police. *Dr Jekyll and Mr Hyde*

STAGE 5 • 1800 HEADWORDS

... future continuous – future perfect –
passive (modals, continuous forms) –
would have conditional clauses – modals + perfect infinitive ...

If he had spoken Estella's name, I would have hit him. I was so
angry with him, and so depressed about my future, that I could
not eat the breakfast. Instead I went straight to the old house.
Great Expectations

STAGE 6 • 2500 HEADWORDS

... passive (infinitives, gerunds) – advanced modal meanings –
clauses of concession, condition

When I stepped up to the piano, I was confident. It was as if I
knew that the prodigy side of me really did exist. And when I
started to play, I was so caught up in how lovely I looked that
I didn't worry how I would sound. *The Joy Luck Club*

Persuasion

JANE AUSTEN

Retold by Clare West

At nineteen Anne Elliot refuses an offer of marriage from Frederick Wentworth, persuaded to do so by Lady Russell, a friend of her dead mother. Wentworth is a sailor, with no money and an uncertain future, says Lady Russell – just a nobody, certainly not worthy of a baronet's daughter.

Eight years later Wentworth returns, a rich and successful captain, looking for a wife. Anne is still unmarried, but Captain Wentworth clearly prefers the company of the two Musgrove girls . . .

Jane Austen's tale of love and marriage is told with humour and a sharp understanding of human behaviour.

The Songs of Distant Earth and Other Stories

ARTHUR C. CLARKE

Retold by Jennifer Bassett

'High above them, Lora and Clyde heard a sound their world had not heard for centuries – the thin scream of a starship coming in from outer space, leaving a long white tail like smoke across the clear blue sky. They looked at each other in wonder. After three hundred years of silence, Earth had reached out once more to touch Thalassa . . .'

And with the starship comes knowledge, and love, and pain.

In these five science-fiction stories Arthur C. Clarke takes us travelling through the universe into the unknown, but always possible future.